DEEP
In The Shallow
End

By

Audra Johnson

ISBN: 978-1-105-66441-0

Copyright 2012 © Audra Johnson

Scriptures taken from the Holy Bible, New International Version®, NIV®. Copyright © 1973, 1978, 1984, 2011 by Biblica, Inc.™ Used by permission of Zondervan. All rights reserved worldwide. www.zondervan.com The "NIV" and "New International Version" are trademarks registered in the United States Patent and Trademark Office by Biblica, Inc.™

Acknowledgements

I wish to thank my family at Cherry Hills Baptist Church. Your love, friendship, support and straightforward Bible teaching played a big role in some major healing. God sent me to you for many reasons, and I will be eternally grateful.

To the small group of magnificent young women who inspired this book – I wrote much of this book based on struggles I knew you faced, but there would be nothing to write if you hadn't overcome them! I love you so much and am so proud of you all. Happy Graduation, class of 2012!

This book is dedicated to my loving parents, Keith and Marilyn Johnson. I can't pay you back for all you've done for me, but maybe this is a start. I love you!

Preface

I'm going to just say it now. Jesus is everything. Above all else. Above all people. Above all ideas and opinions. Above your friends. Above your teachers. Above even your parents! Above sports. Above choir and band and the spring musical. Have I struck a nerve with anyone yet?

You may already recognize this to be true. But do you live it?

For most, summer equals tremendous freedom. You don't have to be stuck in a classroom from 8:15 am to 3:15 pm. You don't have to rush right out to volleyball practice or basketball practice or to a bus to get to an away game, or to do your nine hours of nightly homework. If you're lucky, you don't even have to get up very early! You can spend your days at your leisure, hanging out with friends, swimming, and maybe making some money at a summer job.

Because of this freedom, summer is also the time when the church calendar starts to fill up quickly. The months of June, July and August fill to the breaking point with all kinds of fun. Maybe you volunteer to help out at a Vacation Bible School. Maybe later on you go to a camp...or two...or three. Maybe you even get to go on a mission trip with your youth group or other church members. And scattered in between all that fun are loads and loads of movie nights, sleepovers, and if your church is anything like mine, one or two messy outdoor events that end with really gross stuff in your hair and caked on your clothes.

No other season of the year is as chock-full of things that are designed to bring you closer to God, and closer to your Christian friends.

But eventually, it ends. Your alarm clock rings, and soon after, so does the first bell of school. You burst through the doors fresh, ready, and excited about a new year of living for the Lord. You've been soaked through and through with spiritual renewal, and you can't wait to live it out among your peers. This year you *will make a difference.*

But during the school year, your time is claimed by three thousand activities. Your surroundings include things of this world, rather than things of God, and your social circles probably consist of fewer and fewer of those you worshipped with and served with over the summer, and more and more those who may not even share your love for or even belief in the One True God.

Every year I was in high school, I had the same experience. Every year I was certain things would be different, that the "camp high" as it's widely known, would last through May finals. Every year, it didn't. Every year, I was a fish out of baptism water, being tossed back into my high school where I barely had any Christian friends at all, and my church was 30 minutes away. It's a losing battle...right?

I don't believe that things are supposed to "feel" the same way when we are surrounded with those who don't pursue the Lord the way we want to. It's not a good idea to expect them to. We're told clearly in God's Word that we are to be "in the world, but not of the world." And the world doesn't know God (I John 1:3). So the thing to do is ask ourselves, ask God, ask each other, "how do we keep that deep connection, that deep passion, that deep overwhelming and life changing excitement?" It'll look different, it'll feel different, but it can still be there.

Who better to look to for an example than Jesus Christ Himself? He left His throne in heaven to come down here and dwell in the mess our sinful selves had made of His earth. He had the ultimate "camp high," and He chose to share it in the ultimate "mainstream, secular school." He did it willingly, and maintained His sinless nature and love throughout His ministry here.

This book will take you through four weeks' worth of daily scripture, encouragement, questions and journal space to help you discover practical ways to stay deep in the shallow end of the year.

Working in or Walking With?

Day 1

Read: I John 1-2:17

"This is the message we have heard from him and declare to you: God is light; in him there is no darkness at all. If we claim to have fellowship with him yet walk in the darkness, we lie and do not live by the truth. But if we walk in the light, as he is in the light, we have fellowship with one another, and the blood of Jesus, his Son, purifies us from all sin." 1 John 1:5-7

In life, we have different amounts of money, respect, talent, friends, family and many other things. But every single person has the same amount of time – 24 hours per day. And how we divide up those hours says a lot about who we are and what we value.

Whatever you value most in life becomes your priority. It's natural, and there's really no arguing that fact.

If you wrote everything you did during a given week, from minute to minute, including homework, video game-playing, Facebook, sports, etc., you'll see what your true priorities are. Not what you tell your church group, and not even what you think they are or want them to be. But what they *actually* are.

If I were to do this, I would *think* that my week's priorities would look like this

God
Church/church activities (choir, youth ministry, young adult group, deaconess board)
Family
Writing
Fitness/working out
Work

But in the end, it would look more like this:

Housework
Sleep
Work
TV
Online gaming (yes, I'm a nerd)
Facebook
More Housework
More Sleep
More TV

Believe it or not, I'm not going to ask you to give up anything on your schedule. That's between you and God. But I will give you this takeaway statement:

Time management should NEVER involve "working in" time with the Lord, but "walking with" Him.

This day's devotion isn't about encouraging you to carve out time for one-on-one worship of God through prayer and the study of His Word. That'll come later. If there's only one thing you get from this month of devotions, know that if your entire life, each day, each second isn't fully immersed in the pursuit of the Glory of God now, you're setting a dangerous precedent for the rest of your life.

You'll read a lot of quotes that I still remember my friends in my old high school youth group saying. They've stuck with me over the years.

One night on a mission trip, a friend of mine was leading our group devotion time. He was certainly a representative of the "overly busy high school student and athlete" club. During his devotion, he gave us a great way to think about making Jesus Christ our priority. He had us make a mental list of our activities, interests and responsibilities, and try to arrange them in some sort of order. Given that we *were* on a church-endorsed mission trip, I'm sure that "God" was #1 for most of us.

But that's not the way our list should go, he said. "God should be #1, #2, #3, #4 and #5." In point, **God shouldn't just be at the top of the list, He should *be* the list.**

When we receive God's Holy Spirit, we can't help but to be inundated with His presence. *"Whether you eat or drink or whatever you do, do it all to the glory of God."* – I Corinthians 10:31

To the Glory. For the Glory. Because of the Glory.

It's the only reason we entered this world, and the only thing we'll care about as we leave it. The Glory of God, of His Son, and what we did for them both through His Spirit. Makes you want to take a second look at that list, doesn't it?

At your stage of life, I'm sure you're already thinking your time is not your own. School demands a good seven hours a day, not counting homework, zero hours, sports before or after school, play practice, fundraising car washes, meetings, possibly even detention! Every waking moment of your life is claimed by this teacher or that coach or that history book, and even your sleeping moments get claimed too, as the eight-hours-of-sleep-per-night rule becomes absolutely laughable. I'm horrified at the idea that high schoolers (or younger!) are pulling the sacred "all-nighter" traditionally trademarked by the overwhelmed college student.

And we haven't even mentioned church yet! After the exhilaration of the summer camp, both students and youth pastors are renewed with a fresh vision for their group, which usually involves the rattling off of one event after another. Committees are formed.

Bible studies are chosen. Nights on the calendar are filled up until...conflict. And who wins? Usually school.

So let me challenge you to do this. Claim your education for Christ. Name it. Put a stamp on it. Live it every day.

What do you view as your priorities in your life, right now?

Be honest. If you actually recorded everything you did for an entire week, what would you really spend your time on?

12

Is there anything you do in your free time that you would consider praying about reducing or eliminating in order to free up time to focus more on God?

If so, what would you do with that time?

Journal

14

The Sword Of Truth and "Good Ideas."

Day 2

Read: Hebrews 4:12-13, Ephesians 6:17

You've probably encountered at least one Jehovah's Witness. If not, I'm guessing your parents have. They visit neighborhoods, physically going from door to door asking to share their faith with those inside houses and apartments.

There's a particular woman who canvasses my neighborhood and has seemed to wish to target me, despite my informing her that I am a born-again Christian and if she persists, she'll get witnessed to right back!

Her first visit to my house led to an interesting observation on my part about her approach to the Bible. As she spoke, she pointed to the book she was cradling in her right arm, and told me "we want others to take a look at the Bible. We think it's full of some pretty good ideas about how to live our lives and raise our families today."

Well, all true things. But it's this casual view of the Bible that has placed it on the dusty bookshelves of many Christians – even those who attend church twice per week and serve on committees and maybe even attend a youth camp!

The Bible is God's chief form of communication with us – His church. Yes, He uses music, other believers, and renowned speakers in church and at camp. But the Bible is for us to not only study together, but read passionately alone to reach a better and deeper understanding of God. In the Bible is wisdom. In the Bible is God's personality. His powerfully displayed love and mercy to His people. His expectations. His story. Our story.

Knowledge of the Bible is knowledge of God Himself and of the faith we have. And both knowledge and wisdom come through a consistent, daily committed time in the Bible. All of it.

I'm a fairly ambitious person. I rarely back down from a challenge. When my church offered a "Read the Bible in 90 Days" class, I jumped at the opportunity. It didn't sound that hard – 12 pages a day, to be read in just a short time slot of 45 minutes! No problem.

I was fine the first day, the second, and mostly okay for the third. But the reality of my busy schedule crept in, and soon I found the "simple" task of reading the Bible more and more daunting...then nearly impossible...then impossible. I fell farther and farther behind, while getting more and more frustrated with my failure. Seeing the backed-up pages grow each day, I began to see the project as futile. I'd have to read for a week straight just to catch up! So I stopped reading altogether. My main lifeline to the throne of God had become a personal pet project, and one I was really bad at.

God can speak to me much more powerfully in ten minutes of time that is all His and mine every day than He can in two hours one day, then nothing at all for weeks.

I don't care how busy you are, you have time to spend with your Creator. You'll never convince me otherwise. No, you're not the exception. No, the activity you do at school that you consider a ministry to other kids is not a replacement for your one-on-one time with the Lord. No, leading a small group of middle schoolers at church, working in the nursery, or even planning a Bible study is. Not. The. Same. As. Spending. Time. With. God. This is time you will have to *make*. It will not be given to you.

For most of the remainder of these four weeks, you'll read a little bit from me, but then you'll be given something far more worthwhile. You'll be given one or two Scripture verses or passages to read and a question or two to answer, then some space to journal. This can be a reflection on what you've read, or maybe a space to jot down some things you want to pray about, or maybe just a space for you to write something to God. It doesn't matter to me; you do whatever is on your heart at the time. But you must do this every day.

Just try it...little, time-manageable spoonfuls at a time. I hope you'll soon find yourself craving big ol' shovelfuls of this Book that is the wellspring of life, not just a book full of "good ideas."

In doing this, you show you are serious about bringing the deep commitment to Christ you had over the summer into the not-always-so-Godly school year. The feelings won't last, but your commitment can. It's up to you.

How do you view the Bible? As a guide? A good book with interesting stories?

How much time do you currently spend in reading, studying and meditating on the Word?

19

What items from your schedule could change to make more time for the Bible?

Journal

21

The Healthy, Holy Addiction

Day 3

Read: Deuteronomy 11:18-21

"Fix these words of mine in your hearts and minds; tie them as symbols on your hands and bind them on your foreheads. Teach them to your children, talking about them when you sit at home and when you walk along the road, when you lie down and when you get up. Write them on the doorframes of your houses and on your gates, so that your days and the days of your children may be many in the land the LORD swore to give your ancestors, as many as the days that the heavens are above the earth." (Deuteronomy 11:18-21)

Did you know the Word of God is addictive? It's craveable. The more I read, the more I want to read. The more I learn of the history of God's people, the more I want to learn about their hearts and the situations and circumstances they faced. When I come across a prophet or a disciple, an apostle or a one-mention Bible figure I relate to, I want to know more. I have to know more. God speaks to me, and obviously I want to hear Him.

I went to a Christian college, so once per week I had to attend a Wednesday morning chapel service. However, once per semester, chapel was held for three consecutive days for a good old-fashioned revival. A special guest speaker visited us and spoke in the crowded sports complex.

During one of the revivals, our speaker was a wild-haired older man who played the piano like a maniac, but would randomly and abruptly to talk to us throughout the hour.

The first day of the revival, he excitedly told us he wanted to introduce us to his best friend. I looked around, expecting an equally crazy-haired and spastic guitarist, or maybe a very patient and tolerant wife. Instead, he held up his Bible. "This is my best friend, and has been for 20 years."

The Bible was paperback, worn, torn with pages falling out. The book was stuck half open due to constant turning of pages and neon-colored notes sticking out every which-way. The binding was worn to nothing. The cover showed tremendous weather-fading and age.

This book had gotten some use.

I sat there, watching him expertly turn to any verse he chose in mere seconds. I looked down at my own "best friend." Pristine, shiny, fresh-from-the-factory, just out of the plastic. Barely cracked open, turning the crisp pages took effort, and I had yet to make even the smallest highlight.

There's certainly nothing wrong with a new Bible. But I decided right then and there that my best friend would rival his someday. I wouldn't dare trade it in for a newer model until I had to. Until the pages fell out. Until the binding came loose. And though I've bought different Bibles for different reasons since then, I still use the one I had then. And it is showing a little wear, though not as much as I want.

You can't call someone your best friend if you don't spend time with them. If you don't know them inside and out. If you aren't familiar with their heart.

Whatever your Bible looks like, and even if you get a new one every year – is it in your heart the way it was in the speaker's heart? Do you spend time in it every day, wishing you had even more time with it? This week, devote yourself to spending just a little more time in the Word of God, and see if it makes you crave it.

What does your daily time in the Word look like? Do you journal? Make notes cards for verse memorization? Do you rush through it, or spend time meditating on what you've read?

Think about your favorite way to learn and remember things in school. How could you make this work in your Bible Study time?

What is your favorite book or section of the Bible? Why is it your favorite?

Journal

Just Be It

Day 4

Luke 10: 38-42

As Jesus and his disciples were on their way, he came to a village where a woman named Martha opened her home to him. She had a sister called Mary, who sat at the Lord's feet listening to what he said. But Martha was distracted by all the preparations that had to be made. She came to him and asked, "Lord, don't you care that my sister has left me to do the work by myself? Tell her to help me!"

"Martha, Martha," the Lord answered, "you are worried and upset about many things, but few things are needed—or indeed only one. Mary has chosen what is better and it will not be taken away from her."

A few years ago, I joined my church's youth ministry as a small group leader for a decidedly NOT small group of active, energetic and Spirit-seeking high school freshman girls. This book is largely inspired by their plight through high school, and I felt honored to lead (but more like follow) them through their four years of challenges in faith, personality, choices and pressures.

When the girls were sophomores, I was already well aware that they were pretty extraordinary. Not only did the group not shrink in size as high school progressed, as is the norm, but they grew. New friends were added to our roster every few weeks. The girls eagerly took on leadership roles right away, and actively participated in all group discussions and as many activities as they could.

But of course, we quickly noticed something. The schedule of a teenage Christian can get weighed down and filled up pretty quickly (in case I haven't mentioned that yet!) It's normal, and wonderful, to get easily wrapped up in using your freedom and grace in Christ to serve Him and others. Trust me, I'll never discourage this. Use your youth while you have it to serve our Savior with all your energy! The problem is, though, that we can quickly get caught up in "doing" a relationship with Christ, rather than making simply "being" a child of His. So we came up with a motto for our small group. Similar to the popular Nike slogan "Just Do It," we declared that we would make it a point to "Just Be It."

It's crucial at any point in your Christian walk, but particularly early on, to establish a habit of taking regular time away from work and service and activity to just be with the Lord. I'm not even talking about a daily Bible study and prayer time. I'm talking about just sitting in the presence of Jesus, and doing whatever is needed at that time. Praising Him. Sitting in silence, asking for His peace. Crying. Basking in His love. Whatever that day requires, do it. BE it!

If you don't? What are you risking? From experience, I will tell you. You run the risk of:

- Complacency
- Pride
- Burnout
- Weakened knowledge of Him and His Word
- Possibly even ignoring or forgetting God Himself, and why you love and worship Him in the first place!

Poor Martha has been given a bad reputation in our churches. She wasn't doing anything wrong...exactly. She wanted her house in order, the food well-prepared, everything to be exactly as expected, not only because it was her social requirement, but I thoroughly believe she put forth her effort to honor her Jesus.

And when Jesus went to her to correct her, notice He did not say "Martha, Martha, you sinner! How dare you clean your house and fix the food and then yell at your sister?" Instead he said "Mary has chosen what is *better*."

Mary chose what was better! Jesus was there! In her presence, in her house! She knew how to respond to that. Sitting at His feet, soaking it in. Right where we all should be, all the time.

Christian service, though wonderful and commanded of us, can take away from our time and desire to sit at the feet of Jesus, listen to Him and worship Him. We choose what is good. Time and time again. Today, Jesus is asking you to choose what is better...to Just Be His.

Today, take 15 minutes (or more if you can!) and just sit in God's presence, thanking Him for his goodness and mercy, meditating on His Word, singing, or whatever you want/need to do! If you feel you have anything to write in today's journal, go for it. If not...that's okay! Just Be His.

Journal

The Four Soils

Day 5

Matthew 13:1-9; 18-23

That same day Jesus went out of the house and sat by the lake. Such large crowds gathered around him that he got into a boat and sat in it, while all the people stood on the shore. Then he told them many things in parables, saying: "A farmer went out to sow his seed. As he was scattering the seed, some fell along the path, and the birds came and ate it up. Some fell on rocky places, where it did not have much soil. It sprang up quickly, because the soil was shallow. But when the sun came up, the plants were scorched, and they withered because they had no root. Other seed fell among thorns, which grew up and choked the plants. Still other seed fell on good soil, where it produced a crop—a hundred, sixty or thirty times what was sown. Whoever has ears, let them hear.

"Listen then to what the parable of the sower means: When anyone hears the message about the kingdom and does not understand it, the evil one comes and snatches away what was sown in their heart. This is the seed sown along the path. The seed falling on rocky ground refers to someone who hears the word and at once receives it with joy. But since they have no root, they last only a short time. When trouble or persecution comes because of the word, they quickly fall away. The *seed falling among the thorns refers to someone who hears the word, but the worries of this life and the deceitfulness of wealth choke the word, making it unfruitful. But the seed falling on good soil refers to someone who hears the word and understands it. This is the one who produces a crop, yielding a hundred, sixty or thirty times what was sown."*

I hate to be depressing, but most Christian camps are a perfect picture of these four soils sitting next to each other.

Within any group you'll find the student to hears the message but isn't guarded, and Satan takes the seed of truth from them almost immediately. You'll find the student who responds solely on emotions and the excitement of the camp experience, but never roots into their own genuine faith. You'll find the student who likewise responds to the emotion and feels confident in the setting of being surrounded by Christian friends, but whose faith fails when tested by the outside world. And then, of course, you have students who take to heart what they hear, read, see and experience and, with or without emotion, apply it in such a way that it lasts in their lives well beyond the pomp and circumstance of the "camp high."

I bring this up in the section about time with God because no matter what soil you are planted in, you won't grow and produce fruit to your highest potential unless you are consistently feeding yourself with the Word of God and time in His presence.

As you go into the weekend, I want you to take some time today to think about your youth group, kids you met at camp, even your friends at school and how they relate to each of the four soils. I don't want you to necessarily categorize them or name names, but I want you to spend time in prayer and write down how you can be an encouragement to students in each of these four soils. How can you reach out to those on the path so that they might be willing again to hear the Word? How might you encourage and pray for those on the rocky soil who have simply been caught up in emotion? What can you do for those among the thorns whose faith will be instantly shaken by the world? And how can you come alongside and challenge those in the good soil, where faith is true but will still face the world at every turn?

Weekend Journal

The Path

Rocky Soil

Thorny Soil

Good Soil

With Authority

Day 6

<u>Luke 19: 28-40</u>

After Jesus had said this, he went on ahead, going up to Jerusalem. As he approached Bethphage and Bethany at the hill called the Mount of Olives, he sent two of his disciples, saying to them, "Go to the village ahead of you, and as you enter it, you will find a colt tied there, which no one has ever ridden. Untie it and bring it here. If anyone asks you, 'Why are you untying it?' say, 'The Lord needs it.'"

Those who were sent ahead went and found it just as he had told them. As they were untying the colt, its owners asked them, "Why are you untying the colt?"

They replied, "The Lord needs it."

They brought it to Jesus, threw their cloaks on the colt and put Jesus on it. As he went along, people spread their cloaks on the road.

When he came near the place where the road goes down the Mount of Olives, the whole crowd of disciples began joyfully to praise God in loud voices for all the miracles they had seen:

"Blessed is the king who comes in the name of the Lord!"

"Peace in heaven and glory in the highest!"

Some of the Pharisees in the crowd said to Jesus, "Teacher, rebuke your disciples!"

"I tell you," he replied, "if they keep quiet, the stones will cry out."

"Sing with authority! You are believers! *You have the right to command the worship of your God!"*

Our worship choir quietly exited our practice room to a stage rehearsal following that rousing challenge by our director.

Except me.

I turned to my neighbor and whispered "I have never heard that before! Wow…..I'm writing that down."

I love powerful words. I'm inspired by them. I have a mental list of my favorites, and when I think about them, I'm always tempted to drop what I'm doing and start writing. "Authority" and "Command" have been added to that list.

I have authority. I can command.

It's difficult sometimes to see ourselves as having any kind of authority or the ability to command anything of anybody. If you're reading this, you're probably a high school student. If you are a high school student, you are under the authority of a plethora of people. Your parents. Your teachers. Your coaches. Your supervisors at work.

It's natural to feel as though you are under everyone else's thumb, waiting for instruction or correction or discipline or worse. Waiting to be "commanded."

Therefore, the idea that your life in Christ gives you authority may come as a surprise. It did to me.

But what is this authority?

You are Jesus' representation on earth. You are His creation, superior to the trees and grass and mountains that declare His majesty just by being.

So should you. As the Lord's most treasured created being, you have not only the authority, but the responsibility to reflect Him and inspire others to follow Him in such a profound manner that this inspiration manifests itself as a command.

I wish I had that inspiration in high school. Sure, I tried my best to live for Christ. I was pretty forward in my faith for a shy girl. But I lacked a little bit in understanding my role.

In my community, most of us kids were raised in church. Many of us even made it as far as a middle school youth group. But when high school came, only the "religious nuts" survived. A lot of the kids seemed to view churchgoing as a hobby — like soccer or ballet or Girl Scouts. Just another weeknight activity to quit when they outgrew it.

I've not run into another situation more critical for a solid Christian witness than in high school. Your peers are faced with the same worries and choices that you are, and are beginning to separate from their upbringing and discover their personal idea of "truth." Opinions will form, personal and religious paths will be explored. You are needed to be a representative of the Jesus whom many of your peers know of, have maybe prayed to, but have a great chance of deserting and never truly and fully knowing.

This book will touch on your social life as a recharged follower of the Lord. How will you stay strong when you leave your group of church friends and become immersed in a different crowd? How will you cultivate your friendships with other Christians, whether they sit next to you in biology or go to school 45 minutes away? And how will your view of your classmates change as you learn to look at them the way Jesus does?

Journal

Accountability

Day 7

<u>Acts 2:42-47; John 17, Proverbs 27:17</u>

Proverbs 27:17 – "As iron sharpens iron, so one man sharpens another."

You can have all the motivation you want to make changes for the new school year, but if you don't apply practical principles to your life right away, it just won't work.

As much as I would sometimes like to, (okay, usually), I can't do this alone. I need the fellowship, friendship and spiritual support of others in His church.

"Let us not give up meeting together, as some are in the habit of doing, but let us encourage one another – and all the more as you see the Day approaching." – Hebrews 10:25

If you are not currently in the process of sharpening another piece of iron, do it. I'm not talking about discipleship – I'm talking about encouraging, challenging, and walking beside someone who is on the same path as you.

In school, you'll have to strike a delicate balance between remaining loving, caring, and Christexemplifying friends with your unbelieving crowd, and staying strong and tight with those who profess and live for Jesus. This won't be easy. But to live out the year in the Spirit you are so excited about in the summer, you need others to lift you up...and sometimes hold you up. Your friends will either push you toward Christ or pull you away. While I'm not suggesting you immediately dump every friend who doesn't know the Lord, I am encouraging you to evaluate each individual friendship. Is that person pulling you away from the Lord? Assuming they know you are a growing Christian, do they respect that? Do they hold back from trying to get you to do things you don't want to do? Or do they serve as a snare or a stumbling block for you walk?

Make it a priority to enrich your social life by doing the following:

1. Prayerfully and humbly ask the Lord to make known to you any friends or acquaintances that are toxic to your life in Him. Pray for guidance on how to handle these relationships
2. Strengthen ties with your youth group and any other friends at school (or out of school) that know the Lord.
3. Find an accountability partner.

You've probably heard that term before, but let's look at what a good accountability relationship means.

This person should be someone whom you trust completely and without question. This is someone you will confide in quite a bit. You'll open up completely about your walk with Christ, your struggles with sin, your relationships with others. You'll challenge each other to stay in the Word daily, make prayer and church attendance a priority, and to witness to and serve others, among other things.

Why do this?

We are all accountable to God, today and at the Day of Judgment. Having someone to have to answer to now, directly and in the flesh, is a great way to refine our spiritual lives and protect us against backsliding and the temptations of the world.

In high school, I met with my two accountability partners once a week, right before youth group. We opened in prayer, and asked one another a series of questions:

1. How many days did you spend time in the Word, including reading, journaling, and/or meditating on it?
2. Did you work on memorizing a verse or passage?

3. What did you get out of the sermon this week at church?
4. Did you truly worship the Lord in church, without allowing distractions?
5. Did you struggle with lust?
6. Was your speech godly and edifying to others?
7. How was your thought life this week?
8. Were you a good representative of Jesus at work/school?
9. How did you respect and love your parents, siblings, bosses, teachers, significant others, etc.?
10. Were you a good steward of your finances this week?
11. How can we pray for each other in the coming week?

This list is certainly not all-inclusive. While the core of it should be the basis for your accountability partnership feel free to tweak it to you and your partner's specific situations and needs.

A few more tips on accountability:

1. **Don't mix genders**. Yes, I know. You have a close and fully platonic friendship with a guy or girl. You think that there's no risk in being their accountability partner. Please know that this is far too risky of a game to play. Maybe you are certain you and your boyfriend or girlfriend are

in love and will always be together. Maybe so, probably not. But while you are not married to that individual, you need someone of the same sex to hold you accountable not only in the other areas of your life, but in that dating relationship as well. You'll open up so much to this person, about things that only another guy or another girl can truly understand. You don't want to be in a position where you have spilled your soul to an ex, more than you already have. The horror...oh dear, the awkward horror.

2. **Be accountable to being accountable**. Stick with it. This obviously only works if you actually do it.
3. **Pick someone who is roughly of the same spiritual maturity as you.** Everyone needs a "Paul," a "Timothy," and a "Barnabus." Someone to mentor them (Paul), someone to mentor to (Timothy), and someone to walk beside and support (Barnabus). Accountability will work its way into each of these wonderful relationships, but your "Barnabus" will relate more easily to your current needs and be able to pray for you and support you in very distinct ways.
4. **Finally, choose someone who won't put up with (or worse, excuse) your nonsense**, who, as one of my pastors says, will tell you when you have spinach stuck in your spiritual teeth, but who won't take the place as almighty judge and

jury, either. One of my all-time best friends, Michelle, saw me at my lowest and ugliest point, and loved me through it. She didn't stand by and let me self-destruct, but instead gave me honest counsel. She didn't make it worse by gossiping to other friends or passing prideful and completely unhelpful opinions in my direction, but helped me clean up my mess with a servant's heart and just the right amount of her signature sarcastic humor. I credit her with being the truest of true friends. I know that if I ever slip into that mode again, even though we are hundreds and hundreds of miles apart, I will feel I owe her an explanation.

You don't have to be the social butterfly of your school or youth group, but relying on others to strengthen you and keep you walking strong on the path of the Lord is absolutely critical. If this kind of network doesn't exist for you, spend the next few days and weeks praying about how you can change that.

Journal

Payback

Day 8

Luke 14:7-14

"When he noticed how the guests picked the places of honor at the table, he told them this parable: "When someone invites you to a wedding feast, do not take the place of honor, for a person more distinguished than you may have been invited. If so, the host who invited both of you will come and say to you, 'Give this man your seat.' Then, humiliated, you will have to take the least important place. But when you are invited, take the lowest place, so that when your host comes, he will say to you, 'Friend, move up to a better place.' Then you will be honored in the presence of all your fellow guests. For everyone who exalts himself will be humbled, and he who humbles himself will be exalted."

Then Jesus said to his host, "When you give a luncheon or dinner, do not invite your friends, your brothers or relatives, or your rich neighbors; if you do, they may invite you back and so you will be repaid. But when you give a banquet, invite the poor, the crippled, the lame, the blind, and you will be blessed. Although they cannot repay you, you will be repaid at the resurrection of the righteous."

I love this passage. It's a command straight from Jesus. In just a few short sentences, the Lord asks his followers (us included) to go completely against the world's view of how people should be regarded.

The World's View:

The wealthy first. The powerful. Those with status and possessions and perhaps a solid family name. The polished. The stylish, the well-connected are always first in line. They sit at the heads of tables and are praised and spoken kindly to – usually because their admirers feel that they can reward them for their praise. The wealthy and strong can do things for the "right" person.

Jesus' Command:

Jesus is sharing a challenge to us to go against the world's behavior. Look down to the foot of the table. Who sits there? The common. The ordinary – the middle-of-the-road. Jesus is asking us to love, care for, befriend, and welcome to our table those who cannot pay us back. To invest time in people who can do nothing for us in return. Who are these people to you? Maybe a particular loner or new kid or unpopular kid at school. Maybe someone in your youth group who no one talks to.

Wherever you are on the social totem pole of your school, this is your responsibility. Part of a thriving Christian life is loving and befriending "the least of these." That includes peers who are left out of the crowd. Those who are ignored. Those who are bullied or made fun of, or simply feel nonexistent. Jesus wants you to share His good news of salvation with everyone – the loved and unloved, the happy and the hurting, the girl in the spotlight and the guy who lurks backstage. It doesn't have to start with a big move, just something simple, like inviting someone to your lunch table or slipping a note of encouragement in someone's locker.

Who do you know that you can "invite to the banquet?" Pray about some ideas for what you can do to reach out to them.

Journal

The First

Day 9

Today you are going to read about three groups of people in Jesus' earthly life, from the very beginning to the end. Read each of these passages and write down anything you learn about these groups. Who are they? What do you think their position in society is? What is their connection to Jesus? And what do they all have in common?

Luke 2:8-20

Matthew 4:18-22

Matthew 28: 1-10

    The shepherds were the first to learn of the birth of Christ – not wealthy scholars.

    Fishermen were the first to be called by Jesus into ministry – not the religious elite.

    Women were the first to learn that Jesus had risen – not rulers or His brothers or even His disciples

    God chooses whom He will to do what needs to be done, whenever He decides that person is ready. It's not up to us, and certainly not up to society (praise God!)

You, as a young student have such as tremendous opportunity to make a major impact on not just your peers but on your family, congregation, community, even the world. It may not seem like it, but when teenagers speak up, adults listen. God loves calling young people to His purpose.

Paul urged Timothy to not be discouraged by his youth (1 Timothy 4:12), but to use it for the glory of the Lord. To be empowered by it.

If I added a fourth group to this list, "young Christian people," what would you say about them? What mark are they making on the lost world today? What obstacles are they facing? What is their position in society, what is *their* connection to Jesus? And you, specifically...what are you being called to do today?

Journal

Where you are

Day 10

Weekend reading: (It's a lot! Feel free to just pick one, or split this up over a week or so!)

Esther 4

Exodus 3-14

Joshua 6-12

      As I've written this book, I've served a group of high school women as one of their small group leaders. I've watched them begin high school with excited trepidation and guided them as they experienced all four years of one of the most challenging periods of life. As I write Day 10, my girls are less than four months away from graduation. So naturally, for the past year or so, we've talked and prayed about college! College choices, scholarship applications, roommates and majors. I've told some of my stories that have entertained and downright scared some of them to death (Hahaha!) and they've shared with me their impatience in reaching the next phase of their life.

      A trend now in their conversation is how ready they are to "just go to college." They're *done* with high school! They're so over the tests and drama and impossible teachers and stress and feeling like imprisoned children. I get that. I was there.

It made me think, though, about how I've wasted some precious moments of life by thinking that way too much. By wanting to advance to the next level, I've missed some amazing opportunities on my current level. Wherever you are, there are people to reach, things to learn, and ways that God can speak to you. Don't miss them. While you should prepare and be excited for whatever lies ahead, a lot of that preparation exists right where you are.

Moses had to go through it (along with some very impatient Israelites). So did Esther. So did Joshua. Each was in a position or a task that seemed like it was taking forever. Sometimes God was silent, other times He gave instructions that didn't make sense. Moses had to perform acts that caused plague after plague on the Egyptians. Joshua had to lead the Israelites into battle after battle until not one, not two, but thirty-one kings were defeated. Esther had to risk her life just to speak to her husband about saving her people's lives!

What strikes me in reading all of these stories is that God cared very much about where these people were right then. He supplied for their everyday needs. We're not just chess pieces in a great game of battle that God is playing. We're His children, and he wants us to live a full, satisfying, godly life while we're here. We have a wonderful, indescribable and mysterious future ahead of us in heaven, but this life holds so much as well, and we should take every opportunity we have, no matter what stage it is. Even if it is your last day of high school, use it as only a high schooler can to honor God. It's where you are.

Journal

He Is Willing. Be Clean

Day 11

Matthew 8:1-3

When Jesus came down from the mountainside, large crowds followed him. A man with leprosy came and knelt before him and said, "Lord, if you are willing, you can make me clean." Jesus reached out his hand and touched the man. "I am willing," he said. "Be clean!" Immediately he was cleansed of his leprosy. Then Jesus said to him, "See that you don't tell anyone. But go, show yourself to the priest and offer the gift Moses commanded, as a testimony to them."

This man is sincere in his desire to have Jesus heal him. He doesn't doubt the Lord when he says "if you are willing," he's instead recognizing Christ's sovereignty. He knows and trusts in His power. And he surrenders himself.

This is what we ought to do. Recognize Jesus' sovereignty, trust in His wisdom, put our faith in His ability to heal our hearts and surrender. This isn't just done at your moment of salvation. This is a daily event. Each day, come in surrender to He who just a few verses later, calms a violent lake storm. Who healed those who traveled from all around and asked with pure hearts. Who willingly carried the cross up a hill to suffer for all people. He's still there, ready to heal and make clean all those who come to Him.

What, if anything, keeps you from fully surrendering to Jesus today specifically?

What do you have to bring to Him that needs healing?

Journal

"Dear Papa G..."

Day 12

Matthew 6:5-13

This salutation is usually followed by a chorus of stifled giggles as my group of high-school girls circle up to close our time in prayer. One of the young ladies who is usually the first to volunteer to lead in prayer typically chose the casual approach by addressing God as "Papa G."

I love it. While prayer is certainly something to be approached with sincerity and reverence (you ARE communicating with the Most High, after all), there is no need to be stuffy and inhibited. The curtain is torn. You may approach your Lord as you are. That's what He wants!

Pray your spirit: There are times when I pray a little more formally if that simply is the state of my spirit at the time. For example: just this morning, after I survived yet another round of layoffs at my temp job, I prayed thanks to the Lord, using words like "sustenance" and "provision." Tonight, my talk with God may be just that – a talk. As though I was talking to an old friend over a cappuccino.

God wants your true soul laid at His feet when you pray. Whatever that means. Expose your anger. Reveal your doubts, confess your sins. Think about that!

If a large component of prayer is confession of sin, why would you be afraid to be real in your spirit? Talk to God as you would a human…who just happens to be your Creator. He does deserve the utmost of respect, but wants your humble spirit as it is. He wants to talk with you.

Another benefit of praying like this is the frequency with which we'd pray. Prayer like this is like striking up a conversation with someone who is just always there. You don't have to sit, prepare, and ramble on a bunch of long words. You just start talking.

When the curtain was torn, we were granted total access to the Lord. No longer did approaching the throne have to be preceded by washing, sacrificing, and the wearing of sacred garments or by being the "correct" person. Jesus' blood gave us what we needed to be with God, not just in heaven, but here.

So saying you don't have time to pray is like saying you don't have time to think or talk to a friend. In the time it took you to send that last text, you could have praised God, confessed a sin or two, or asked him to help you through some trial you're facing. They don't have to be long, drawn-out ordeals. God is always there. Talk to Him like He is.

Instead of answering questions today, I want you to spend today's time in prayer, and if you feel so led journaling. Some people like to pray in the written word (myself included!) If not, just spend a little extra time talking with God.

Journal

Basket case

Day 13

<u>**Mark 6:30-44**</u>

The small boy stood in awe at the noisy crowds surrounding him. Men, women and children just like him swarmed about, but the boy did not know why. The air was hot from the noon sun. A rumble through his stomach reminded this young boy that it was lunchtime, and he was to return home as quickly as possible with the fish he had caught that day and the barley loaves he had purchased for his family as part of his chores.

Just as he turned to leave, a low, kind voice inquired of him, "Do you think you could help me?"

The boy turned cautiously, not particularly wanting to disobey his mother and speak to someone he did not know. But the face before him was so kind. The man was smiling and his eyes bore into the boy's in such a manner that it almost seemed like this man knew his thoughts.

"Well...I need to run home to bring this food to my family," the boy stammered.

"Actually, that's what I need. You see, there are thousands of people here, and it is time to eat, but I don't have any food to give them, nor do any of my friends." He pointed to a group of frustrated, squabbling men who looked like they could use a change of clothes and a bath. "And, I'm sure you can tell we certainly don't have enough money between us to feed all these hungry people," the man laughed.

The boy knew what the man was getting at. "Well, sir, I have food, but not enough to feed everyone. I have five small loaves of bread and a couple of small fish I caught this morning. Not nearly enough for everyone; it's barely enough for my own family!"

The man continued to smile. "I promise you, if you trust me and help me out, your family will not go hungry."

The boy was shocked. How did he intend to feed everyone with this small basket of food, and still have enough left to give to his family? Not wanting to disappoint the man, however, he consented. "It's not much, sir, but you can have it."

The man thanked him and departed to return to his friends. Their incredulous expressions made the boy smile as the man described his plan to them. Suddenly, the man bowed his head as if in prayer, and began distributing food. He did not stop. Every time someone reached into the basket, they took as much as they wanted for themselves and their family. The basket was passed and passed and passed, and the food never ran out. Everyone ate and laughed and talked until they could eat no more. The man's friends began to walk around with baskets, picking up whatever the crowd did not eat. By the time they were finished, the boy had counted twelve full baskets!

The man approached the boy once more, and presented him with a large basket of food. "Take this to your family, and thank you for providing me with what I needed." And the boy returned home with twice the food he had obtained himself.

How much is in your basket? How much do you have to give to Jesus? Maybe not much. Some days, maybe even less than five loaves and two fish.

We're not talented enough, smart enough, kind enough or knowledgeable enough to do anything for the Kingdom of God. But He is. He is powerful enough to do anything He wants, but He asks one thing. He wants back the resources He gave to us in order that we might glorify Him, and He needs us to be willing to give them over no matter how insignificant we think they are. I believe that God wants nothing more of us than to go to Him with our little baskets and say, "It's not much, Lord, but it's Yours. Do what You want with it." Not only will He take what we offer, but if He wills it so, He will feed thousands upon thousands with it.

Journal

The Trick

Day 14

Read: Psalm 8, Psalm 103, Psalm 139

    Service can be exhausting, even if done with the purest of hearts. It's essential to keep your life in balance when devoting it to the Lord. He wants you to work for Him, but understand that while we're in our mortal human selves, we wear out, physically, mentally, even spiritually.

    You may have heard the term "burnout" before. It's serious business. It's not just a little fatigue or boredom due to overworking yourself...the effects can last for years, or even your lifetime. Worldly thoughts crowd your mind, pushing out your dedication to following the Lord and doing His will.

    I experienced burnout after my junior year of college. I seriously overloaded myself that year. I was a Resident Assistant in my dorm, editor of our campus newspaper, and taking a very ill-advised 21 credit hours. Add to that the heartbreak of losing out on a youth internship I wanted terribly, the heartbreak of losing a boy I wanted terribly, and subtract any real social life a normal 21-year-old should have, and you have a very clichéd recipe for disaster and burnout.

    My final camp story takes place shortly after this year ended. I was deep into burnout. I had been pelted with disappointment, frustration, loneliness and over serving without allowing myself to be spiritually fed. I wasn't part of a campus Bible study, I no longer had an accountability partner, and I was barely going to church. I felt that my leadership and service elsewhere made up for it, without realizing that that same leadership and service was impossible without being fed spiritually by a church family or group of like-minded peers.

Despite not getting the youth internship I wanted, I still volunteered to attend one of my favorite camps with the middle schoolers, whom I was working with over the summer. I loved this camp. Equal parts fun and Biblical challenge, craziness and conviction, all with trust and a conspicuous lack of rules. (I'm a big rule person, but I loved how this camp simply trusted the church groups that attended!)

Our role as adults this week was pretty simple: be there. Hang out with the kids, make sure to keep a lid on chaos and mutiny, attend kids with injuries (which happened frequently!)and pray for and with them as needed. This usually happened at night, during the all-camp worship services.

My favorite perk of being an adult at this particular camp was the blessed ability to enter the worship center before the kids could. Though I loved it for the air-conditioning, the purpose was to pray. We'd find our section of chairs, and spend some time sitting in them or walking past them, praying for the students who would soon sit in those chairs. Each night was a powerful opportunity for the kids to make decisions for Christ, or to respond to a call to ministry, or commit to sharing their faith with their friends or family. They were powerful and emotional moments, and we prayed fervently that the students wouldn't let anything hinder them from responding.

I walked among the chairs one night, and was suddenly urged to sit down in the middle of a row. I had no idea who would sit in that chair that night, but I knew God was telling me to pray for them, right then, right there. I wondered if it'd be the girl who hadn't spoken a word all week and was clearly unhappy to be there, or one of the boys who was struggling with being bullied at school. Maybe it was the girl who was wondering if God was calling her to missions. Regardless, we adults were there two purposes right then: pray and be available. No matter our skills or backgrounds or histories or mistakes, we worked together to pray for a fantastic group of kids. It was the first time in months I felt fulfilled, fed and necessary. All because of prayer to my God. Best job ever.

It was communion night. Everyone's favorite. It occurred midweek, and instead of opening the gates and letting 300 screaming teenagers flood into the room, the kids would walk in solemnly, taking in the candles scattered on the stage, the bread and juice resting in stately trays on tables in front, and the soft music played by the band. Communion would be served by the kids and adults going up to the elements as they felt led, taking it for themselves, then taking some back to serve whomever they chose. It was a pretty special event.

Somberly, the kids walked in, and without word, found their section by looking for the adult faces familiar to them. I was impressed that our group walked in as one, and not in little cliques. They filled in the rows intently and began to settle in.

The speaker began to give a short devotion that would lead up to the time of communion and worship through singing. From the looks on their faces, I could tell that every single one of the kids was fully prepared, except for that one possibility…where was she? I looked up and down the rows to find her. It should have been an easy task, as the adults were asked to sit on the ends of the rows so as to have a better eye to keep on their group. Except that night I had…

A wave of total conviction and total awareness of God's no-kidding-around serious love flooded my heart. I couldn't help it. I started to cry.

I was still sitting in the seat I had prayed over.

I can tell you firsthand that the person who would sit in that chair that night was truly in need of prayer. She had been doing all the right things for all the wrong reasons, and it had torn her heart. Her actions of service without taking the time to fill up on the Word of God, communication with Him, and true fellowship with his Church wasn't selfless and strong, it was stupid. Just plain foolish.

It's a pretty sad day when God has to trick you into praying for yourself, isn't it?

Balance in our lives is crucial. We're not perfect servants, and we won't be able to serve nonstop flawlessly until Heaven. We're still in our training pants here on earth, and we have a lot to learn. We simply can't pour our whole selves into service if we're not willing to commit to learning why we do it. To striving to work side-by-side with others. To sharing our burdens and taking on shared burdens in return. To gaining wisdom from those who have more of it, and humbly accepting instruction from those called and equipped to give it. To simply enjoying the company of fellow believers every now and then! To resting when it's time to rest, and working when it's time to work. To taking very special care of ourselves and the bodies we've been blessed with to do His work.

You have a ton of demands on you right now, without even having to add any of your own. What areas of your life are lacking? Pray today and this week to get them back into balance, evening things out with more of what you need and maybe a little less of something else.

What areas of your life are being neglected? (Academic/studying, social life, physical well-being, relationship with God)

What areas of your life may be a bit too full?

List some ideas for ways you can even things out to achieve a balance

If you were to say a five-minute prayer for just yourself, what would you pray for?

Journal

Search Me

Day 15

Read: Psalm 139

I'm praying that in the course of this book, you've realized that there are days when you crave nothing but a time of spiritual renewal and refueling. Sometimes, even our Bible study can become part of our to-do list as we discussed earlier.

Today, if it suits you and where you are, I encourage you to read Psalm 139. Read it more than once. Pray it, meditate on it, and maybe even try to memorize it. Journal your thoughts about it as you read. Some of you won't need or want any time of guide for this – you'll just want to write. But if you want some words to prompt you, use the guided journal I have written.

Vs. 1-6 – Write a few sentences about how you feel about God knowing you so well. If this makes you nervous, perhaps write a prayer expressing that to God, and asking Him to show you the comfort and confidence that comes from being in touch with the God who sees us.

Vs. 7-12 – Have you ever wanted to flee from God? Do you ever wish there was a way you could hide something from even Him? If so, confess this and ask Him for forgiveness and assurance in that forgiveness.

Vs. 13-16 – Thank God for the way He made you, both physically and mentally. Reflect on the beauty He gave you, and how you are truly created in His image.

Vs. 17-18 – Thank God that He is always thinking about you and loves you. Is this easy or hard for you to recognize?

Vs. 19-22 – David takes quite a turn at this point in the psalm! In the middle of worshipping God and meditating on His love for him, David turns to a cry for justice for those against him and against God. This is a beautiful picture of how we are able to be in total praise and adoration of our Lord, while suffering from all our earthly struggles. They can coexist. What are you struggling with now that you would consider your enemy? Is it hard for you to continue to worship God in these circumstances?

Vs. 23-24 – These are two of my favorite verses in the Bible. After praising some characteristics of God and worshipping Him, then expressing anguish about everything that was bringing him down, David ends his psalm with a request and commitment. He asks the Lord to purify him of anything displeasing or unholy. He trusts the Lord to know him well enough to do this, and faithful to carry it out. Write a prayer similar to David's, but in your own words, asking God to search you and refine you so as to be a better servant to Him.

Pew-climbing rebel

Day 16

Luke 19:1-10

Jesus entered Jericho and was passing through. A man was there by the name of Zacchaeus; he was a chief tax collector and was wealthy. He wanted to see who Jesus was, but because he was short he could not see over the crowd. So he ran ahead and climbed a sycamore-fig tree to see him, since Jesus was coming that way.

When Jesus reached the spot, he looked up and said to him, "Zacchaeus, come down immediately. I must stay at your house today." So he came down at once and welcomed him gladly.

All the people saw this and began to mutter, "He has gone to be the guest of a sinner."

But Zacchaeus stood up and said to the Lord, "Look, Lord! Here and now I give half of my possessions to the poor, and if I have cheated anybody out of anything, I will pay back four times the amount."

Jesus said to him, "Today salvation has come to this house, because this man, too, is a son of Abraham. For the Son of Man came to seek and to save the lost."

I'm no rebel. I never have been. I always obeyed my parents and teachers, with nary a question as to their authority or common sense. I feared getting into trouble. When in first grade, I even cried all the way to the principal's office, even though I knew he had only called me there to return my jacket that he'd found on the playground.

But I've had one delightful moment in my life where I very much went against what I was told…and I do not regret it one bit.

I was twenty years old, and spending my fifth year at a weeklong church camp. But this wasn't your ordinary church camp. I called it "evangelical discipleship boot camp." It was a pretty serious deal, and only a few chosen ones were supposed to be selected to go by their youth pastors. But over the years, that hadn't been followed as well, and a wide variety of kids showed up.

This was my fifth year at the camp and second as a Team Leader over a small group. This year, I had students getting ready to go into their senior year of high school. I have to say, the week was not a good one. I was sick with what later turned out to be a severe sinus infection, so I basically felt awful with few actual symptoms. My "school" was the smallest of all of them, and the kids adapted to the camp week a little differently than usual. Instead of warming up to the group and opening up and sharing around mid-week, they started in immediately with intense revelations and confessions, some of them pretty serious, and some of them falling into the category of "Way Too

Much Information." And this all happening on Monday night. I was a little unprepared for that! And though I had never had a problem before, I just didn't click with my "family group" of students or many of the other Team Leaders. And especially not the dean of our school. He showed very little signs of like or even respect toward me. I wanted the week to be over ASAP.

I wasn't alone. One girl (whom I will call Allie) stood out from the others. Literally. She wouldn't join any sports or activities, never spoke in family group time, and caused problems during the lessons, like laughing, goofing off, drawing all over her guide book and getting her friends to do the same.

We tried to get her involved and interested for a few days, but it just wasn't happening. She noticed the negative attention she was drawing, and it made her worse. She even wandered off during one recreation time, which of course I got blamed for. I was instructed to be on her like white on rice, never letting her out of my sight. This obviously infuriated her, and she shut down completely.

During one of our team leader meetings, our dean shared with us that he had attempted to get her sent home. He had just had enough, and didn't want to distract the other students who wanted to be there. I understood his point, but totally disagreed with him. He then revealed that he wasn't able to have her sent home, because her parents were on a 6-week summer cruise, and this was her fourth week of various camps she had been shipped off to. So there was nowhere to send her.

Any other light bulbs going off?

Of course she's acting out, I thought...she's being forced into drama camp, dance camp, volleyball camp, and some random "Jesus" camp (in her eyes). She didn't want to be there, but couldn't be anywhere else.

Our direction was, since we were "stuck" with her, we were to ignore her. Pay absolutely no attention to her whatsoever.

That was not something I could do.

I somehow made it to the end of the week. At our final night worship service (usually the most emotional experience of the camp,) I wound up standing right behind Allie. I thought that if any part of this week would touch her at all, it'd be this one. I watched her intently during the powerful time of singing. Nothing. She knew she was on the "ignore" list. That knowledge had made her shrink even more into herself. I was filled with anger, and desperation to not let this week end badly for her. She wasn't someone to ignore, and she needed to know it.

A strong urge came to me...perhaps God talking, or perhaps my emotions getting me carried away. But it was there, and I couldn't ignore it. "Take off your shoes, climb over the pew, and pray with that girl."

Take off my shoes? *Climb over the pew?* WITH THE DEAN WATCHING? He stood only two or three people away from me. I was supposed to ignore her, pretend she wasn't there. I'm not sure what kind of trouble I thought I'd get in, but at that point it just didn't matter. I was in.

I nervously slipped off my sandals and, shaking, hoisted my leg over the pew and catapulted over. (I'm short. There's no more graceful way to make that happen.)

Feeling the heat of curious, suspicious, or perhaps just plain angry eyes coming from the row behind me, I squeezed myself in between Allie and one of her friends, put my arms around them, and began to pray out loud. I prayed for her, thanking God that she'd been brought there and that I had gotten to meet her. I thanked Him for her friends, for her family that allowed her to come, and asked that the rest of her camp experience be blessed. I hugged her and her friend, and slowly returned to my seat. I didn't look our dean in the eye. But my fellow team leader put her arm around me, smiling broadly.

I'm not sure what I expected to happen next. At best, maybe in just a few short minutes Allie's heart would be changed and she'd run to the altar in tears, asking Jesus to come into her heart. That didn't happen. Maybe I thought she'd show a glimpse of interest in the Word being spoken to her. Nope. Nothing.

Later that night, I exhaustedly entered my dorm room and began to pack up. I was really ready to leave! My eyes surveyed my room and landed on the pile of snacks I had brought. A pack of juice boxes, some crackers, and a bag of Dove chocolates. I had been too sick to eat much of it. Smiling, I gathered them up and headed across the hall to Allie's room.

It was around midnight, so when I knocked on the door, I was met with stone silence. They weren't asleep, I knew, but they most likely thought I was coming to yell at them to quiet down, or maybe it was the female administrator coming to deliver a fate worse than death for their lights being on past "lights out." The door squeaked open, and Allie and her roommate looked at me in utter fear. (Seriously, the penalty for even the slightest rule violation was something to drive fear in the hearts of the most rebellious of teenagers.)

I smiled. "Hi girls," I said quietly. "I was cleaning out my room and didn't want these to go to waste." I held out the chocolates. "Want to share?" Relieved smiles and excited nods all around.

For the next hour or so, we ate and talked. Not about anything spiritual, but just about whatever they wanted. Boys. Clothes. School. More boys. I learned a lot of gossip about the male side of our camp!

Suddenly, another knock at the door shut us up. We looked at each other in panic. I was about to tell the girls I'd take the heat when the door opened, and the other two female Team leaders for our school appeared.

"Hi," I said sheepishly, "we were just ….snacking."

They smiled, and seeing how involved Allie was, nodded approvingly at me. "Can we join?"

I don't think Allie left that camp a saved-by-grace human being, a new life in Christ. Maybe she did. But I do know that she left there with a good memory of fun and laughter, and not just a week full of bad memories and exclusion. She had one person purposefully reach out to her, even when told it was wrong. That's probably all we could hope for, and I believe it was only reason I was there. She was my Zacchaeus. Jettisoned from polite society, stamped with strict warnings not to bother trying, all she needed was a tree to climb. But like Jesus, I refused to do what society said, and like Jesus, I dined with her (on a healthy meal of chocolate and juice boxes).

You know you have a Zacchaeus at school. I'm betting you even have one in your youth group. Who is he? What is she about? How can you climb up that tree, or over that church pew, and get to know them, and try to draw them in?

Journal

Inimitable

Day 17

Exodus 7: 8-24

The LORD said to Moses and Aaron, "When Pharaoh says to you, 'Perform a miracle,' then say to Aaron, 'Take your staff and throw it down before Pharaoh,' and it will become a snake."

So Moses and Aaron went to Pharaoh and did just as the LORD commanded. Aaron threw his staff down in front of Pharaoh and his officials and it became a snake. Pharaoh then summoned wise men and sorcerers and the Egyptian magicians also did the same things by their secret arts: Each one threw down his staff and it became a snake. But Aaron's staff swallowed up their staffs. Yet Pharaoh's heart became hard and he would not listen to them, just as the LORD had said.

Then the LORD said to Moses, "Pharaoh's heart is unyielding; he refuses to let the people go. Go to Pharaoh in the morning as he goes out to the river. Confront him on the bank of the Nile, and take in your hand the staff that was changed into a snake. Then say to him, 'The LORD, the God of the Hebrews, has sent me to say to you: Let my people go, so that they may worship me in the wilderness. But until now you have not listened. This is what the LORD says: By this you will know that I am the LORD: With the staff that is in my hand I will strike the water of the Nile, and it will be changed into blood. The fish in the Nile will die, and the river will stink; the Egyptians will not be able to drink its water.'"

The LORD said to Moses, "Tell Aaron, 'Take your staff and stretch out your hand over the waters of Egypt—over the streams and canals, over the ponds and all the reservoirs—and they will turn to blood.' Blood will be everywhere in Egypt, even in vessels of wood and stone."

Moses and Aaron did just as the LORD had commanded. He raised his staff in the presence of Pharaoh and his officials and struck the water of the Nile, and all the water was changed into blood. The fish in the Nile died, and the river smelled so bad that the Egyptians could not drink its water. Blood was everywhere in Egypt.

But the Egyptian magicians did the same things by their secret arts, and Pharaoh's heart became hard; he would not listen to Moses and Aaron, just as the LORD had said. Instead, he turned and went into his palace, and did not take even this to heart. And all the Egyptians dug along the Nile to get drinking water, because they could not drink the water of the river.

Moses and Aaron had something to prove. Pharaoh's heart was hardened toward God and the Israelites and wouldn't acknowledge the Lord's authority and the certain destruction that would befall his nation if he didn't at least consent to the release of God's people.

But for the first few tries whatever the brothers did, the Egyptian magicians and sorcerers could do the same, and because of that (and an insurmountable pile of stubbornness), Pharaoh refused to heed Moses' warnings, and the Israelites remained trapped.

I'm not sure how they did it…maybe it was an optical illusion. Maybe it was some sort of demonic invocation. Maybe it was even God Himself. But I'm always filled with a little bit of disappointment and frustration for the visiting team, the Israelites. I can't wait for God's power to be so obvious and undeniable that Pharaoh, fearfully trembling, sends the Lord's people away. But not only does he not, at first…he has no reason to! His own magicians are adding insult to slavery by mimicking the miraculous acts!

Our actions can be imitated. Our good deeds, our love and concerns for others, so much of what is supposed to make us stand out from the crowd is easily (and genuinely) repeated by those who don't have Christ in their hearts.

We have to go beyond. Love the way no one else knows how. Act when no one else has time (or courage). See the hurt that no one else can see, and reach out with the grace of your Savior when all others fail. Be there when everyone else has left. Show up when no one else cares enough to. Prove that there is a driving force, an everlasting conviction, an all-encompassing and soul-shaking love whose effects are superhuman. Make them ask you why. Live for Christ in a way that can't be mocked.

Journal

Standing Strong

Day 18

Read: Matthew 28:20, Luke 10:16, I Peter 4 12-19

I'm not proud of this one.

By my senior year of high school, I was finally experiencing the blessing of having supportive Christian friends both in and out of school. One place, however, where I was still alone was my history class. Most of the other kids in that class were friends, and part of the elite "preppy" crowd. They spent nearly every class period terrorizing our teacher, making fun of her behind her back *and* to her face, and making miserable the life of anyone who would dare stand up for her. They'd argue with her and debate the validity of her lessons until she broke down. It wasn't a pleasant hour-and-a-half of my day. Unlike my other classes, I was pretty content to just sit in the back corner and be invisible.

Which is why I was quite uncomfortable on the day she passed out the blank white index cards.

"We're going to do an experiment, "she announced with unusual excitement and confidence. "On these cards I want you to write three words or phrases you'd use to describe yourself. Any three words you want."

I held the small white card in my hand, and instantly knew my choices. "Christian. Writer. Family." The three most important things in my life.

But when I picked up my pen, I couldn't bring myself to do it. Christian? Did I actually dare write THAT? Fear of a certain social doom got the better of me. I was very open about my Christ-following. It wasn't a closely guarded secret, but somehow, knowing these would probably be read in class...to THIS class...was a little too much.

I scribbled down something else to replace "Christian." I don't remember what it was. Obviously it wasn't that important.

The teacher collected the cards (which were not signed) and in fact did begin to read them aloud. "Basketball...music...good friend. Acting...popular" (Yep.)

After reading most of the cards, she smiled, satisfied with the results. "You'll notice," she said, "that no one identified themselves according to whether they're male or female, their race, their nationality, or their religion."

Oops.

She continued. "That's just not how we see ourselves, is it? That's not how we identify ourselves to the public. We're more than those labels...."

As my small-group girls would say today, "Epic fail, Audra."

What a chance I had! That's not how I see myself? Of course it is! After being life-changed by the grace of Christ, that's ALL I wanted to see in myself! That's the ONLY way I wanted to be identified. And so many others would agree! Ugh. How could I have missed the boat on that one? I was furious with myself. And the ironic thing is, had I disproved my teacher's theory; I probably would have won the favor of my peers even more.

I was rather surprised at myself for letting this intimidation stop me.

What's stopping you? Even if you stand strong for Christ every day, can you identify any thing or person or situation that might block you? Is it something you can or should prayerfully consider removing from your life? And if not, what can you do to stay strong? Take the weekend to visually go through your entire week and identify times when it's harder to be a Christian. Pray about how you can turn those times around and live for Him better than ever.

If someone filled out an index card about your identity, what three words/phrases would appear?

Do you find all your identity in Jesus? If so, how does it show to others? If not, why not?

Journal

The Color Purple

Day 19

As we begin to wind up this journey, I want to leave you with my favorite camp moment. It's hard to choose, as you've read some moments that I hope have struck some kind of nerve in you. But the moment I'd return to if I could is a rather short one...just a few moments.

In the summer of 1998, as an 18-year old recent high school graduate about to dive into the ultimate transition of college life, I spent a week at the "evangelism boot camp" I talked about a few days ago. As I said then, each group at the camp consisted of a large group of kids from each grade, 7th through 12th. Except for the Purple Group – my group that year.

The Purple Group was dwarfed by the larger, louder, more face-painted groups. We were tiny, a bit more reflective, and a little more serious. Instead of being grouped according to our age, we had chosen to take part in this different team. We were seven boys and eight girls who had been called to full-time ministry.

Over the camp's five days, we learned what it was like to be the Acts 2 church. We ate together, learned together, worshipped together, and though separated by gender and an acre of campus, stayed in the same rooms at night. For that week, I was closer to these 14 other teenagers than anyone else I had ever met.

The week wasn't without struggle, for any of us. When you have that tight of a group in such a safe setting as a church-based camp, stuff will come out. We shared all sorts of deep issues such as abusive pasts, sexual histories, fears, and family obstacles. Though we had spent every waking minute together, we were still essentially strangers, so revelations of this kind took a lot of trust and comfort with each other. We were a family with a shared cause.

The final all-campus worship service of the week went beyond all my expectations of an emotional, Spirit-filled, spine-tingling event. All fifteen of us had battled demons wanting to stop us, and with each others' help had crushed barriers and broken down walls. Some of us felt exalted, ready to worship and praise God with all that was in us. Some of us had been broken, devastated by sin, resistance, or evil influences. Some were struggling against what God wanted to reveal to us that week. We were fifteen people, in fifteen completely different spiritual places, on varying levels of the mountain or valley.

Our posture in worship that night proved it. Some of us were standing, arms raised to the Lord. Some of us were sitting, crying. Some were sitting with heads bowed in prayer. Some were kneeling before their chairs, praying. Some were even laying on the ground, sobbing. Fifteen people, in different places, feeling different things, showing it in different ways, but in absolute connect to the same loving God.

    And we were there together. I'll never forget this picture. No matter if we were standing, sitting, laying, or jumping up and down on a chair, we were connected, literally. Some hands held other hands, some hands were laid upon their neighbor who was in a different place spiritually and in the room. Some were lifted high. Some were comforting someone in pain. I can't imagine a more accurate picture of the Church.

    When the bus pulls into the church parking lot, and you sleepily unload your suitcase and pillow, you should expect that, though it may seem as though your youth group is on one very high level, they're not, and certainly won't be when school starts. You have different friends, different classes, different expectations, and different callings within your school. So you will feel different things. At some times, you'll be standing on that chair while your neighbor sits beside you weeping. Sometimes you'll be sobbing on the floor while your best friend stands nearby in joyous praise. Sometimes that kid you don't know very well will need your arms around him or her, praying for them as though you know their very heart. Be prepared for it.

Journal

A Good Friday

Day 20

Good Friday. Around me, dozens of my fellow churchgoers quickly filled the aisles. This wasn't the end of a service; no one was buslting toward the exit. They were lining up to receive the Lord's Supper at the end of our candlelight service. Nearly a dozen of our pastors and elders stood at the front holding the gleaming, felt-lined trays of cut-up bread and tiny plastic juice cups. Behind them, chartreuse-carpeted steps led up to the stage where we could kneel and pray.

I'm usually not a fan of the "go up as the Spirit leads" variety of communion. Usually the congregation waits for that first brave soul to step out, then the mass crowd rises and rushes to the front like it's an all-you-can-eat shrimp buffet. But this evening I didn't get annoyed. I sat back and watched as families went together to take the elements. Husbands serving their wives and mothers serving their children. I watched as young couples knelt and prayed together arms around each other's backs. I watched as elderly church members made their way up with canes and walkers to worship their Lord they had loved for decades. And I thought back to when I too worshipped that freely. Troubled perhaps, but not burdened by bitterness. When I worshipped not just through my tears but with them. When laughter and heartache approached the throne hand in hand, and I let it show on my face.

• • •

I was dry. For several years I had been dry of spirit. I couldn't get intio worship songs; I wouldn't go near a ladies Bible study for fear of the saccharine falseness I feared so much. I had even found it nearly impossible to serve actively in my new church, even though I loved it very much. I had only recently joined the worship choir, whose presentation that night may have been the only reason I'd shown up for the Good Friday service in the first place.

It wasn't God I was running from, it was His church. I had been hurt. I had been burned. I had been zapped of all spiritual energy. I had made dumb choices, and I had been paying for them, and as a result, I could not emotionally engage myself in worship. I loved the Lord with all my heart; I just didn't *feel* anything anymore.

Pondering this, I made my way up to the front where I took the elements with sincerity, if not emotion.

I knelt on the steps and asked God to forgive my complacency and restore my passion. Then I went back to my seat among those who had chosen to sit and pray in the dimly lit, quickly emptying sanctuary.

It's about Him. Not me.

Gently, God whispered to me the truth of the past few years. I had seen His powerful work on the height of a spiritual mountain, and His healing and provision in the darkest of lows. Now I saw nor felt either. "I wanted to see if you'd be obedient, with or without the emotion." I felt Him say to me.

When the happy spike dulls, when the crisis is over and life returns to normal, your obedience will be tested. Life is good when you're seeing the sunshine; hope is born when you are forced to dwell in darkness. But when life drifts to the middle and goes back to the everyday, you'll be expected to love Him as passionately and serve Him as determinedly as you promised to when your hands are raised to heaven in surrender bathed in the feelings of the camp high. Whatever you said you'd do, you better have meant it! You won't feel like it a few weeks down the road, but your obedience will be tested. You have the tools to make it happen, and the strength of the Holy Spirit to stay Deep in the Shallow End.

Journal